BOROUGH OF TWICKENHAM LOCAL HISTORY SOCIETY

OCCASIONAL PAPER NO. 3

Alexander Pope's Twickenham — 18th Century Views of his "Classic Village"

by

T.H.R. Cashmore, D.H. Simpson and A.C.B. Urwin

April 1988

This book is issued to celebrate the three hundredth anniversary of Alexander Pope's birth, and his residence in Twickenham from 1719 to 1744. It accompanies an exhibition of the same name held in Orleans House Gallery.

"View from Richmond Hill" by Peter Tillemans, on the front cover (see Plate 1) is reproduced by permission of the Government Art Collection. The sketch of Pope by William Hoare, c1741, on the back cover, is reproduced by permission of the National Portrait Ga...

C   Borough of Twickenham

ISBN 0 903341 46 8

INTRODUCTION

Alexander Pope came to Twickenham, where he was to spend the rest of his life, in 1719. The riverside village had had a long history, extending back to Saxon times. Twickenham Park, on the borders of Isleworth, had a number of residents of substance and position, among them Edward Bacon and then his brother Francis in a house built there in 1561/62. The village was increasingly recognised as a convenient spot in which nobility and gentry could enjoy rural quiet within a short distance of London. During the last two decades of the 17th century its residents had included twelve noblemen, a bishop, five titled widows, three baronets and eight knights. Its growth continued in the early years of the eighteenth century, and to the fashionable houses, particularly along the river side, were added the terraces of Montpelier and Sion Rows.

Lady Mary Wortley Montagu, who made a practice of residing during the summer at Savile House from 1719 to 1739, wrote in 1722, "I am at Twickenham where there is at this time more company than in London" and later in the same year commented, with pardonable exaggeration, for the Parish had a population of fewer than 1500 – "Twickenham is become so fashionable and the neighbourhood so enlarged that it is more like Tunbridge or Bath than a country retreat". In 1723 John Macky, a government agent and spy, described Twickenham as a "Village remarkable for an abundance of curious seats".

Pope was a little over thirty when he came to Twickenham, but was already England's most famous poet. He was born in London in 1688, the year of the "Glorious Revolution", into a Roman Catholic family which, as a result of penal laws, moved away from London while he was still a small child. Hitherto a healthy boy, he became seriously ill when twelve years old and grew up puny of stature, much deformed, and a semi-invalid. Despite little formal education, he proved a most precocious child, beginning to compose poetry almost as soon as he could write. His first published poems were *Pastorals* in 1709, and *The Rape of the Lock* followed in 1712; a collected edition of his early works was published in 1717. Famous in his early twenties, he became wealthy through his translation of the *Iliad* into English verse, published between 1715 and 1720. This enabled him to make his home in Twickenham, together with his recently widowed mother and his old nurse, Mary Beach, and to live here with the attendance and comforts that money could provide.

At first he thought of building a house, and the architect James Gibbs provided him with plans, but the cost deterred him. Instead, he bought the lease of an existing riverside house, together with five acres of land; Gibbs undertook the first alterations he made to it. Over the years Pope continued to enlarge and improve the house, and above all his garden, partly between his Villa and the river, but the larger part beyond the road that ran from Twickenham to Teddington and divided his grounds. To link the house with the area across the road he made an underground passage which he converted into his famous grotto. In gardening, in embellishing the grotto, and in the conversion of his house into a Palladian villa, Pope had the help of many friends, in particular Burlington, William Kent, and Bridgeman.

For the rest of his life, spent in Twickenham, Pope wrote mainly satirical and moral poetry. To mention only one work, in 1733, in the fulness of his literary maturity, he published *An Essay on Man,* which discussed in sometimes magnificent verse, the philosophical ideas of his age. This was the source, for example, of "The Proper Study of Mankind is Man" and "Hope springs eternal in the human Breast" and many other well known sayings. It might indeed be said that during his life the whole classical period of British literature centred around him.

Pope's character as well as his verse has caused endless controversy. To his enemies he was an intriguer, spiteful, mean, dishonest, and vain; to his friends he was loving, generous and witty. But sometimes his closest friends could become his bitterest enemies, as was the case of Lady Mary Wortley Montagu, and he could be over-sensitive and waspish.

His literary achievements also brought social success, and with other famous writers he was readily admitted to the highest social and political circles. He enjoyed his success and in Twickenham welcomed the visits of older friends. These included men who set the tone in literature, or the fashion of Palladian architecture, or in garden design – Bathurst, Bolingbroke, Gay, Arbuthnot, and Swift, and the Blount sisters from Mapledurham. There were also many local residents who became acquaintances, friends, or even enemies – they included Sir Godfrey Kneller, Lady Mary Wortley Montagu, Lady Suffolk (whom he advised on the lay-out of her garden at Marble Hill), Lord Strafford, the Vernons, James Johnston, Lord Islay in Whitton, and James Thomson across the Thames in Richmond. Despite his Roman Catholicism, he must also have had contacts with various vicars of Twickenham – in succession Samuel Pratt, Penyston Booth, Daniel Waterland and Edmund Martin. In 1726 a nine-year-old boy visited Twickenham; it was Horace Walpole, who three years after Pope's death was to make his home in Twickenham for the last fifty years of his life and to continue its literary fame, and who in later life recalled with pride, "I have seen Pope".

Throughout his years in Twickenham, Pope, a leading light among the Augustan poets, viewed his villa in terms of a rural retreat from the latter-day Rome. "My Tusculum" he called it, and his presence and influence gave to Twickenham its contemporary title of "the Classic Village".

This booklet is intended to illustrate that village as it was in his lifetime, during the reigns of the first two Georges, and to show as many as possible of the major houses of the period, especially those beside the River Thames. Where possible, original paintings and drawings have been used rather than engravings which have already been so fully and admirably described in Bamber Gascoigne's *Images of Twickenham* (1981) but, where necessary, prints have been used to fill gaps. Though some of the illustrations date from a period after Pope's death in 1744, they nevertheless represent scenes and dwellings that existed during his lifetime. They start downstream, with east Twickenham and the edge of Isleworth, move upstream through Twickenham village and to Pope's Villa, then through the middle of Twickenham and along the road to Whitton, ending with Kneller Hall, and Whitton Park on the borders of Hounslow. A reproduction of part of Rocque's map indicates the location of many of the buildings.

A more comprehensive account of the history of the houses than is given here is contained in *Twickenham 1600-1900: People and Places* (1981).

ACKNOWLEDGMENTS

Our thanks and those of the Twickenham Local History Society go to the owners of the pictures contained in this booklet both for their permission to reproduce them, and their kindness and valuable help. In particular may we thank the Ashmolean Museum, Oxford; the British Rail Pension Fund Works of Art Collection; Jonathan Charlton; the Hon. Lady Cotterell; the Government Art Collection; Michael Ingram; the London Borough of Richmond upon Thames; the Lewis Walpole Library, Yale University; the National Portrait Gallery, London; and the Whitworth Art Gallery, University of Manchester. Our thanks also go to Christina and Bamber Gascoigne and to Jonathan Ditchburn for their kindness in loaning us negatives of certain prints from their *Images of Twickenham* and for permission to reproduce them.

In selecting the pictures we have had the invaluable and ever-patient advice of Patricia Astley-Cooper; and in avoiding the pitfalls of publishing we owe a large debt of gratitude to Roy Massey and our printers, CTD of Twickenham.

The costs of bringing out *Alexander Pope's Twickenham* were beyond the resources of our small Society, and its publication was only made possible by help from several quarters. Thanks must go to John Young of the Ram Brewery, Wandsworth (who keeps alive Pope's memory with the nearby hostelry of "Pope's Grotto"); to the London Borough of Richmond upon Thames; and finally to members of our Society who have supported our Papers for the past 25 years, and once again rallied round at the last moment to help finance this, our most ambitious publication.

JOHN ROCQUE'S MAP OF 1741

John Rocque, a Huguenot, became a noted surveyor, engraver, and publisher of prints in England. His most productive period was between the years 1734 and 1762, and he was for a time "Chorographer" to the Prince of Wales. The detail of Twickenham and the Thames as it was in Pope's time shown here is from his *New and Accurate Survey of the Country round London,* 1741. Though his maps were not based on any systematic triangulation, and may have errors of detail, at least some of the local gardens (e.g. Pope's Villa, Twickenham Park) appear to be reasonably accurate. The map on the opposite page has been marked to show the main sites depicted in the illustrations in this book. The names by which some are more familiarly known are given in brackets.

1. Railshead
2. Twickenham Park
3. Richmond Ferry
4. Ashe residence (Cambridge House)
5. Marble Hill
6. Montpelier Row and Chapel
7. Johnston's House (Orleans House) and Ragman's Castle
8. Lord Strafford's House (Mount Lebanon) and Riverside
9. York House and St Mary's Church
10. Dr Battie's House
11. Pope's Villa
12. Lord Radnor's House
13. Strawberry Hill
14. Present day Twickenham Green
15. Heatham House
16. Kneller Hall
17. Whitton Park and Place

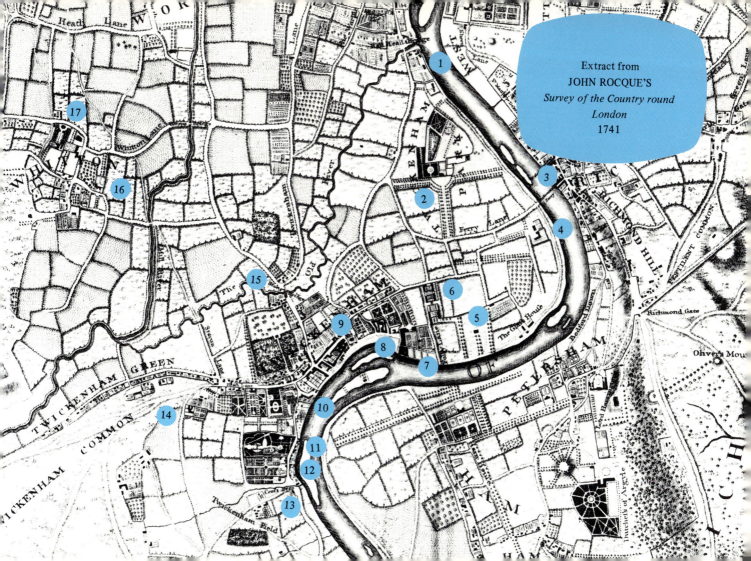

Extract from
JOHN ROCQUE'S
Survey of the Country round
London
1741

PLATE 1

"View from Richmond Hill"

Peter Tillemans — c1730
(Government Art Collection)

This splendid painting, which is reproduced in full on the cover, includes a remarkably accurate panoramic view of Twickenham and the river Thames as far back as the tower of St Mary's Church, with glimpses of the Countess Ferrers' summer house and of Pope's Villa. The bends in the river, however, with a touch of artistic licence, have undergone adjustment to create a sense of balance.

The major Twickenham houses are, from the right: Twickenham Park (residence of Thomas Vernon and, later, of his widow — Pope's landlords): the Ashe family home close to Richmond Ferry (later called Cambridge Park); the two distinct blocks of Montpelier Row recently built by Captain John Gray, with Montpelier Chapel lying between the two; Lady Suffolk's new house of Marble Hill, then, as now, painted white, which was completed by 1729 but not occupied by her until 1735; and Secretary Johnston's house with its newly-built Octagon Room. All the houses and buildings mentioned above are shown, and described in more detail, on later pages.

Tillemans painted two other scenes in this area about 1730; one of the river frontage of Twickenham south of the village (Plate 18) and a view of Richmond across the river from Twickenham Park.

PLATE 2

The Terrace and the view downstream from Richmond Hill

Leonard Knyff — c1720

(London Borough of Richmond upon Thames, Orleans House Gallery)

This painting includes, on the Middlesex bank to the left, the Ashe family house (see Plate 4), and beyond it Twickenham Park (see Plate 6). In midstream is the ferry conveying a coach and horses to the Twickenham bank (see Plate 3). The bridge was not built until 1777. The three houses on the river bank just beyond Twickenham Park (see Plate 7) can hardly be distinguished. The clipped trees on Richmond Terrace can be seen again in Plate 8, and just above them on the Richmond bank is Cholmondeley House, seen also in Plates 4 and 5.

PLATE 3

Richmond Ferry

James Marris — c1770
(In private ownership)

The main means of transport between Richmond and Twickenham before the building of the bridge in the 1770s was Richmond Ferry, which was probably considerably older than its first recorded mention of 1443. Carrying animals and vehicles as well as passengers, it was cumbersome and liable to hazards of winds and currents in bad weather. Joseph Windham Ashe (see Plate 4) was one of the eighteenth century holders of the lease. This pen and ink drawing shows the Ferry nearing the Twickenham bank, with Richmond Hill in the background.

hill & Houses higher

PLATE 4

A view from Richmond Hill looking downstream

Antonio Jolli — c1745

(In private ownership)

This view, painted within a year of Pope's death, deserves comparison with Tillemans's painting (see Plate 1). On the extreme left, on the Middlesex bank, is a long, low building with a cupola, possibly a converted orangery then known as "The Glass House" (also shown on Rocque's map) and above it Twickenham Park (see Plate 6). Next is the Ashe residence, close to the road to the Ferry. Built about 1620 by Sir Humphrey Lynde, it was occupied in the reign of Charles II by Sir Joseph Ashe; his family intermarried with the Norfolk families of the Windhams and Townshends, the latter related to the Walpoles. This Whig connection would not have appealed to Pope. At the time of this painting the house was occupied by Joseph Windham Ashe, a Windham who had married his cousin, the Ashe heiress. He was responsible for major alterations to the old 17th century dwelling, enlarging it and adding a west front. In 1750 it became the home of Richard Owen Cambridge, from whom it took its later name of Cambridge House. Beyond this are the Isleworth Houses (see Plate 7). Across the river on the Richmond bank, close to the Ferry, stands Cholmondeley House (Plate 2).

PLATE 5

The Thames at Richmond, with Cholmondeley House, looking upstream

Antonio Jolli —c1745
(In private ownership)

This is the counterpart to the previous illustration; notice Joseph Windham Ashe's house and the ferry on the right. This view shows the whole of the Richmond Riverside as Pope would have known it, apart from the remains of the Palace just off the picture to the left (Asgill House had not yet been built).

At this time the riverside at Richmond was still a promenade; the towpath was on the Twickenham bank until 1779. This part of the river looking upstream is also seen in a painting by Peter Rysbrack, c1723 (not reproduced here).

PLATE 6

Twickenham Park House;
a detail from Peter Tillemans's "View from Richmond Hill"
c1730 (Plate 1)

Twickenham Park was the largest house in Twickenham, shown as having 37 hearths in the Hearth Tax Return of 1664. The house, astride the Twickenham and Isleworth Parish boundaries, was built in 1608/09 by Lucy, Countess of Bedford, and in 1730 it was still as originally built (Ham House, across the river, was built in 1610). According to Rocque's map of 1741 the Twickenham Park House still had the formal gardens laid out by the Countess. However, in 1722 Batty Langley (born in Twickenham in 1696) had carried out some major landscaping for the then owner Thomas Vernon, and some of the trees he planted are still flourishing. Pope rented his house from Vernon and, later, his widow, and was not able to buy it until she died in 1740. Shortly after this, Twickenham Park House had another storey added between the end towers, and the turret roofs lowered, by Diana Countess of Mountrath. The earliest print of the house did not appear until 1784.

PLATE 7

"A View up the Thames between Richmond and Isleworth"
drawn and engraved by John Boydell – c1755

Three houses were built at Railshead on the Isleworth bank of the river, the name coming from an early fishery here. The land was originally part of the adjoining Twickenham Park (see Plate 6).

The later building on the site of the house on the left was known as St Margarets and gave its name to the area. Governor Pitt (see Plate 11) lived in the central house from 1742 to 1744, but after 1749 it was named after its occupant James Lacy, a partner of Garrick at Drury Lane. The right hand house (now called Gordon House) was built in 1718 by Moses Hart, an extremely wealthy Government stockbroker who lived there until 1757; it still survives, with an addition of 1758 designed by Robert Adam.

PLATE 8

"A View of Richmond, taken near Twickenham"

drawn and engraved by John Boydell — 1753

In addition to showing Richmond Hill (see Plate 1) Boydell depicts a portion of the Twickenham river bank lying between Marble Hill (see Plate 9) where Lady Suffolk was still living, and Cambridge House (see Plate 4) where Richard Owen Cambridge had recently taken up residence. At the time of Pope's death, and until 1779, the towpath for barges (drawn by men) for this stretch of the river lay on the Twickenham shore between Railshead and Orleans House.

The dwelling on the left of the picture, together with its summerhouse, appears in other contemporary prints, and was there in Pope's time. It was subsequently greatly altered or demolished, and replaced by the house later known as Little Marble Hill.

PLATE 9

"The Countess of Suffolk's House at Twickenham"

Augustin Heckel — 1749

(Courtesy of the Lewis Walpole Library, Yale University)

Henrietta Howard, Countess of Suffolk, is more commonly known as the long-suffering mistress of King George II. She withdrew from this unenviable position in November 1734, having had the foresight to have a country retreat built, the Palladian villa of Marble Hill, designed by Roger Morris and Lord Herbert, later Earl of Pembroke. Pope and Charles Bridgeman had a hand in laying out the grounds, whilst Dean Swift wrote witty verses about the house. Lady Suffolk remained a good friend of Pope's, sending him an "Edder-down Quilt" in 1739, which he found "the greatest Comforter I have". Earlier he had written of her in his poem "To a Certain Lady at Court"; Pope thought her "a reasonable woman, handsome and witty, yet a friend". She outlived him, dying at Marble Hill in her eightieth year in 1767.

the Countess of Suffolks House at Twickenham.

Ao 1748.

PLATE 10a

Montpelier Row and the Chapel — a detail from
"View from Richmond Hill"
by Peter Tillemans — c1730 (Plate 1)

PLATE 10b

Montpelier Row — detail from the engraving
"A View of the Countess of Suffolk's House near Twickenham"
by James Mason from Augustin Heckel's original

Plate 10a is probably the first picture of the magnificent group in the north-west corner of Marble Hill Park of two terraces built in the 1720s by Captain John Gray, who then had an estate in Twickenham, and the private chapel between them which he added in 1727. It was ministered by Anglican clergy living in the town or nearby, and in the first years of the nineteenth century the proprietor was Archdeacon Cambridge.

Plate 10b shows an end-on view of Montpelier Row from the river; the engraving is based on plate 9, but this detail does not appear in Heckel's original. Sion Row, a smaller terrace of rather similar houses nearer the village (Plate 13) also dates from the 1720s.

The house occupied by Secretary Johnston and later Governor Pitt,
and view upstream to St Mary's Church

Augustin Heckel — c1744

(London Borough of Richmond upon Thames, Orleans House Gallery)

PLATE 11b

Ragman's Castle — detail from
"Governor Pitt's House (late Secretary Johnson's) at Twickenham

engraved by James Mason, from another watercolour by Augustin Heckel — 1749

Heckel's watercolour possibly predates 1744, and shows the house built by John James in about 1710 for James Johnston (1643-1737), formerly Secretary of State for Scotland and himself a Scot. The Octagon to the left was built by James Gibbs in about 1718, and is linked to the house only by a low wall, later replaced by a single storey link building. Pope had no liking for Johnston, and in December 1730 referred to "my neighbour Johnson's (sic) criticismes which (I verily believe) are as wild in Poetry as in Politicks". After Johnston's death, the house was occupied by George Morton Pitt, a "nabob" with an Indian fortune, who had been Governor of Fort St George and became M.P. for Pontefract. The building was later known as Orleans House after Louis Philippe, Duc d'Orleans, lived there.

Downstream from Johnston's house stood the small building shown in Plate 11b, which during Pope's time was an inn, originally called the "Dog and Partridge" and later "Ragman's Castle", a haunt of bargees, beggars, and the Marble Hill gardener Moody, whose neglect of his duties is recorded by Swift:

"An idle rogue who spends his quartridge
In tipling at the Dog and Partridge".

It was subsequently replaced by the small but genteel dwelling shown which retained the old name.

PLATE 12

"A View of Twickenham"

Augustin Heckel — 1748

(London Borough of Richmond upon Thames, Orleans House Gallery)

This watercolour is the original from which an engraving was made the following year, though some of the foreground details have been altered. St Mary's Church (see Plates 14 and 15) is seen to the extreme left. To the right of the sailing barge is a group of houses including Willow Bank, Aubrey House and the White Swan Inn. Next are the present Ferryside and Ferry House (the latter subsequently much altered) and the large building with a pediment is the house built by Viscount Raby, later the Earl of Strafford, at the beginning of the 18th century. In his absence on diplomatic duties or at his other estates, it was frequently occupied by his mother, Isabella, Lady Wentworth, an assiduous writer of entertaining if strangely spelled letters, who died there in 1733. This was the site of the later house called Mount Lebanon. Samuel Scott painted a similar scene to this, excluding the Strafford house, in about 1760.

A View of Twickenham

At. 1748.

PLATE 13

A detail from "A View of Twickenham"

Edward Ironside — 1786

(London Borough of Richmond upon Thames, Twickenham Library)

Although artistically naive, and painted many years after Pope's death, this watercolour, by the Twickenham historian Edward Ironside, is included since it shows several important buildings as Pope would have known them. On the left is St Mary's Church (see Plate 15); in front of it is the old Vicarage, and to its right Dial House, built by the tea and coffee merchant Thomas Twining in about 1726 and now St Mary's Vicarage. Next is the earliest known picture of York House. This takes its name from a family which owned property in Twickenham in mediaeval times; the present house was rebuilt or substantially altered in the 1630s and further extended at the end of the century; with later additions, it still stands. On the corner of its grounds is Langham Cottage, and on the right the end of Sion Row (see Plate 10b).

PLATE 14

St Mary's Church

Samuel Scott — c1763
(Ashmolean Museum, Oxford)

In the 1760s Samuel Scott lived in the Manor House, in Church Street, and the gate posts of the house can be seen at the bottom of this watercolour. Pope's friend and, eventually, literary executor, Henry St John, Viscount Bolingbroke, had owned the Manor House, but fled to France following the 1715 Rebellion before Pope came to Twickenham. He stayed with Pope in Twickenham for several months following his pardon and return from exile in 1723. His properties had been sequestrated, and his leasehold interest in the Manor was sold by the Commissioners of Forfeited Estates, also in 1723. The Church can also be seen in Plates 11-13 and is described in the note on Plate 15. The Church-wardens' Accounts mention the "Great repair on the Cornish" in 1763, and this appears to be the reason for the scaffolding. To the right, Church Lane leads down to the river; the inn sign of what became known as the Two Sawyers can be seen there.

PLATE 15

"Twickenham on the Thames"

Samuel Scott — c1760
(Whitworth Art Gallery, University of Manchester)

St. Mary's Church and the heart of the village of Twickenham clustered about it are seen from Eel Pie Island. The Church tower of Kentish ragstone is mediaeval, but the corresponding nave fell down in April 1713, and the larger replacement nave, designed by John James of Greenwich, was of red brick and in the contemporary style. Sir Godfrey Kneller, as Churchwarden, took a leading part in raising subscriptions and in the direction of the work (see also Plate 25). Pope designed a memorial to his father to be placed in the Church, leaving room for his mother's name and date of death, and his own, to be added. He also placed a memorial to his old nurse, Mary Beach, on the exterior wall when she died in 1725. Later, a large memorial to Pope by Bishop Warburton was placed in the north gallery, and a modern brass plate now marks his burial place.

The warehouses to the right of the Church, and the anchored barge, are reminders of the commercial use of the river for transport. The flat-roofed building in the centre is Strand House, which still survives. The inn-sign on the left cannot unfortunately be identified.
For a continuation of this view upstream see Plate 16.

PLATE 16

"View of Twickenham"

Samuel Scott — c1765
(Ingram Family Collection)

This watercolour is virtually a continuation of the scene in Plate 15, but looking in the opposite direction along the bank of the Thames towards Pope's Villa, which can just be discerned on the extreme left. The building on the right appears to be a timber yard, and probably adjoined the wooden building seen on the left of Plate 15. On the craft in front of it are constructions which seem to be eel traps. This group of wooden buildings stood in the area which is now the upstream end of the Embankment. The wall in the centre is that of Poulett Lodge (Plate 17). The riverside to the left of the view can be seen more clearly in Plates 17 and 18.

PLATE 17

Dr Battie's House and upstream to Pope's Villa

Augustin Heckel — c1750

(In private ownership)

This watercolour painted from the Surrey bank shows the main houses lying on the river side of the old highway from Twickenham to Teddington, now known as Cross Deep. (It became a turnpike road in 1767.)

The house on the right was built by William Battie (1704-1776), President of the Royal College of Physicians, on the site of one destroyed by fire in 1734. It had a single bay and a broad terrace supported on arches. In 1758 he was succeeded by Vere Poulett (1710-1788) who became 3rd Earl Poulett, and from whom the house derives its customary name of Poulett Lodge. To its left is Cross Deep, another 18th century house, and the only one of its period to survive on this stretch of the river. Next is the domed summerhouse on ground belonging to the Shirley family, whose main property was on the other side of the road.

PLATE 18

"The Thames at Twickenham"

Peter Tillemans — c1730
(British Rail Pension Fund Works of Art Collection)

No precise date can be assigned to Tillemans's magnificent oil painting of the riverside of Twickenham from the Surrey bank, but the extent of buildings shown suggests that it was near the end of his life (he died in 1734). To the left is the Ait in front of what became Radnor House (Plate 21). The next major house is Pope's Villa (shown in enlarged form in Plate 19); to its right is the Shirley summerhouse, and the houses nearest the village (Plate 17); on the extreme right is the Parish Church and the close-packed buildings around it. Tillemans's foreground records the diversity of use of the river for pleasure and commerce, with elegant riders, fishermen, a group of labourers pulling a barge along the towing path, and the varied river craft making up the passing scene which Pope enjoyed watching from the tranquillity of his grotto.

PLATE 19

Pope's Villa — Detail from
"The Thames at Twickenham"
by Peter Tillemans — c1730

Alexander Pope moved to Twickenham in 1719 shortly after the death of his father, and leased a property on the bank of the Thames from the Vernon family. He employed James Gibbs to remodel the house, and he produced a Palladian Villa with a central portion rising to three storeys, and wings a storey lower. This is the only extant view of the house as it was then.

PLATE 20

"An Exact Draught and View of Mr Pope's House at Twickenham"

Engraved by N. Parr from the drawing
by Peter Rysbrack — c1735

In the 1730s Pope added a portico to his villa, as can be seen in this engraving, the only one published in his lifetime. The party disembarking from the boat may be visitors, for Pope allowed his servants to show the gardens to those who wished to see them.

The arch beneath the portico is the entrance to Pope's grotto. Since the major part of his garden, to which he gave so much attention, was on the far side of the road, he had a passage constructed to link the two without the need to cross the highway, and made this utilitarian facility into a feature embellished with rocks, mirrors, pyrites and other items, which he used as a retreat from which the river was visible.

PLATE 21

"The Earl of Radnor's House at Twickenham"

Augustin Heckel — 1749

(London Borough of Richmond upon Thames, Orleans House Gallery)

This is the original watercolour from which a copper engraving was published the following year. On the right is Radnor House, the home of John Robartes (1686-1757) who became 4th Earl of Radnor in 1741. He was Pope's next door neighbour, and the subject of his biting wit in the *Dunciad*. Like Pope, he joined the two portions of his garden on either side of the road by a tunnel. The house was embellished by murals and coloured glass, some of which was damaged by an explosion at the gun-powder mills which also shook Strawberry Hill in 1772. A summerhouse can be seen in the garden. The house to the left is Cross Deep House (not to be confused with Cross Deep, nearer to Twickenham village — see Plate 17).

The Earl of Radnors House at Twickenham *m* *t* *elegant* A. 1749.

PLATE 22

East front of Strawberry Hill
Etched by C. Woolaston — 1754

A small house was built in 1698 on a plot known as Strawberry Hill Shot; it had many occupants, one in Pope's time being Mrs Chenevix, a noted "toy-woman" with a shop in Charing Cross. In 1747 Horace Walpole bought the remainder of her lease, and soon after purchased the property. He eventually transformed the small dwelling into his Gothic castle of Strawberry Hill. This etching shows the first embellishments of the original house. The outbuildings visible to the left, which would have been there in Pope's time, are on the site later occupied by the Gallery and Round Tower.

PLATE 23

"A View taken on Twickenham Common"
Drawn and engraved by John Boydell — 1753

This is the earliest view of the area of Twickenham away from the river. The land in the foreground is the part of Twickenham Common nearest the village: it stretched off to the right towards Hanworth until reaching Hounslow Heath. The animals in the foreground are a reminder of the use of common land for pasturage. The central house was at that time occupied by the 4th Baron Kingston; he had married the widow of the former owner, Admiral Sir Chaloner Ogle (c1681-1750) whose memorial in Twickenham Church is near the Pope memorials in the north gallery. On the extreme left is Twickenham House, later the home of Sir John Hawkins.

Though all the houses in this scene have disappeared, the open space shown largely survives as Twickenham Green, and the track along which the coach is driving is now the Hampton Road.

PLATE 24

Heatham House

Anonymous watercolour — c1750
(Courtesy of the Lewis Walpole Library, Yale University)

Heatham House, on the north bank of the River Crane, was purchased with adjoining brewery by Stephen Cole from Captain John Cruikshank, R.N., in 1736. The Cole family were brewers in Twickenham from the seventeenth to the nineteenth centuries, their original brewery being in the same neighbourhood. Stephen (1707-1790) was a member of the fifth generation of his family to live locally. He was an active participant in local affairs, a J.P., twice a Churchwarden, and a member of the Vestry. He had a large family by two marriages, and bequeathed the business, which had considerably expanded under his direction, to his eldest son, also named Stephen. Heatham House continued to be Cole property for many years, though the family ceased to live in it and leased it to a variety of tenants, and it still survives; the brewery has, however, been demolished and the postal sorting office stands on its site.

PLATE 25

Whitton: the House of Sir Godfrey Kneller

Drawn and engraved by John Kip — c1715

Sir Godfrey Kneller (1646–1723) came to England from Germany in 1676, and from 1680 until his death was principal painter to the court. He built his house in Whitton in 1709-1711 where, wrote Vertue, "he lived in the summer visited and courted by all people of Honour and distinction". He was a Justice of the Peace and became Churchwarden in 1713, the year in which the nave of St Mary's Church fell down. During his three years in this office, he played a major role in rebuilding the Church (see Plate 15). This rare engraving shows an "ideal" view of the estate, but the detail of the house is confirmed by the glimpse of his house in the background of his self-portrait of 1706-1711 in the National Portrait Gallery. Kneller was a friend of Pope's, and painted his portrait, but Pope would not agree to remove his family memorial in Twickenham Church to make way for Kneller's monument and, though he is buried at Twickenham, his memorial was erected in Westminster Abbey.

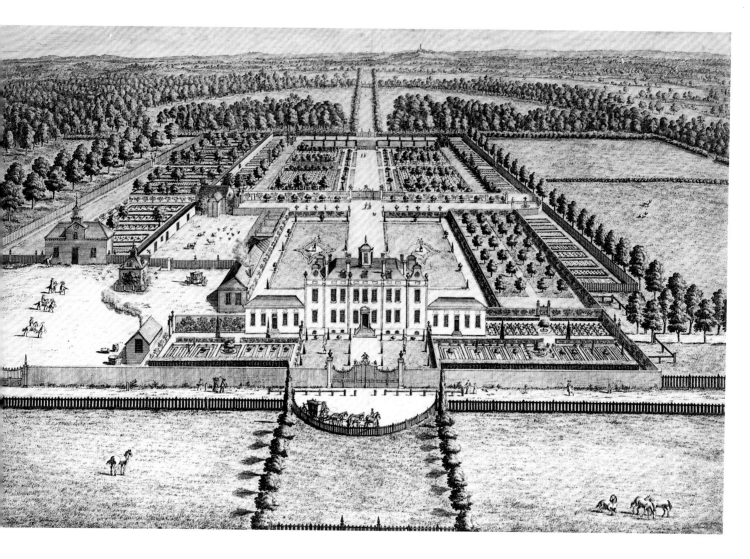

PLATE 26

"A View of the House and part of the Garden of His Grace the Duke of Argyl at Whitton"

Drawn and engraved by William Woollett — c1757

Archibald Campbell (1682-1761), Earl of Ilay and, from 1743, 3rd Duke of Argyll, a powerful and devious politician during the ascendancy of Walpole, began to acquire land in Whitton in 1722 and eventually had an estate of 55 acres which he called Whitton Park. He used it especially for the cultivation of rare plants and trees, some of which were later transferred to Kew Gardens. An important feature, therefore, was a large Green House designed by James Gibbs. To the east of this Ilay had a dwelling house built to a design ascribed to Roger Morris. It was forty-five feet square, flanked by walls which joined it to office blocks and rooms associated with the stock and management of the estate. In front of it was a bowling green.

PLATE 27

"A View of the Canal and of the Gothick Tower
in the Garden of His Grace the Duke of Argyl at Whitton"

Drawn and engraved by William Woollett — 1757

In front of the Green House in Whitton Park (see Plate 26) was a canal-like pond, stocked with carp and tench, which stretched towards a "Gothick" triangular tower (architect unknown) used as a summer house. In this engraving the Duke, wearing an apron, is seen showing a party of guests round his estate. It was later owned by the Gostling family, and the Green House became the basis of their mansion.

SELECT BIBLIOGRAPHY

Victoria County History of Middlesex, Vol. III

Borough of Twickenham Local History Society Papers, particularly No. 47, *Twickenham 1600-1900: People and Places* (1981)

Borough of Twickenham Local History Society Occasional Papers No. 1, *Twickenham Parish, Notes for Students and Researchers* (1979)

M.R. Brownell, *Alexander Pope and the Arts of Georgian England* (1978)

R.S. Cobbett, *Memorials of Twickenham* (1872)

M.P.G. Draper and W.A. Eden, *Marble Hill House and its owners* (1970)

B. Gascoigne, *Images of Richmond* (1978)

B. Gascoigne and J. Ditchburn, *Images of Twickenham* (1981)

E. Ironside, *History and Antiquities of Twickenham* (1797)

D. Lysons, *The Environs of London,* Vol. III (1795)

M. Mack, *Alexander Pope: a Life* (1985)

M. Mack, *The Garden and the City* (1969)

H. Pye, *A short account of the Principal Seats and Gardens in and about Twickenham* (1760)